Offering Meditations and Prayers

Offering Meditations and Prayers

by Laurence C. Keene

Chalice Press
St. Louis, Missouri

©1984 by CBP Press (now Chalice Press)

All rights reserved. No part of this book may be reproduced b
any method without the publisher's written permission. Address
Chalice Press, Box 179, St. Louis, MO 63166-0179.

Scripture quotations, unless otherwise noted, are from the
Revised Standard Version of the Bible, copyrighted 1946, 1952©
1971, 1973 by the Division of Christian Education of the Nationa
Council of the Churches of Christ in the U.S.A. and are used b
permission.

Library of Congress Catalog Card Number:
84-266

ISBN: 0-8272-2706-X

Cover design by Mel Lovings

10 9 8 7 6 5   97 98 99 00 01 0£

Foreword

Fundamental to the religious life is the idea that we are expected to be giving and sharing people! From the very beginning, when gifts took the form of animal and grain sacrifices, to these present days when we use folding money, real estate, and blue-chip stocks to express our devotion to God, an important measure of our commitment has always been our willingness to glorify God by sharing our wealth and blessings with others. When we "take an offering" in our worship services, we are "making an offering" in the same devotional sense as did the patriarchs of old when they selected and gave the very best of their flocks and fields as an expression of gratitude to God.

It is my desire that these brief meditations and prayers--whether they are used in the church paper to encourage stewardship or in the worship service itself--will help to clarify the act of sharing as a treasured, worshipful experience. I make these meditations my offering to those who find them helpful.

Contents

Money Is Power

SCRIPTURE: Romans 1:16

The apostle Paul did not say: "The love of money is the root of all evil." What he said, more accurately, was that "the love of money is a root of all kinds of evils" (1 Tim. 6:10 ASV). We have ample proof of the truth of his statement.

Money is also the root of much good! The great healing and learning centers throughout the world have been created by people with big hearts who have been generous with their money. Money is not a dirty word! It is simply another word for "power." This power can be used for good and noble purposes or it can be used to destroy and corrupt.

Providing you with the opportunity to give to the Lord's work is our way of unleashing the power you have at your disposal for the world's most noble venture!

PRAYER: Eternal God, we know we have not always used our money correctly. We also know we have lost power when we have spent our income carelessly. We don't need more money, but we do need more power in our lives. Focus our giving so that we can feel a renewed sense of your power. In Jesus' name. Amen.

Giving Beyond Hurting

SCRIPTURE: Colossians 3:15

Someone once asked what percentage of one's earnings a person should give to the church. Someone once suggested that we should give "until it hurts." The idea expressed in that statement, of course, suggests that unless a gift is to some degree sacrificial or painful its impact really isn't felt by the giver.

While there may be some truth to this view, it seems more beneficial to think in terms of "giving until it *helps*." We do not give money to the Lord's work to inflict pain on ourselves. While we do sometimes give to reduce the pain and suffering of others, we practice giving because we know that generosity enlarges our character and gratitude for what God has done for us. We also know that our capacity to "inherit the earth" and to enjoy all that God has for us in the world is determined by the size of our gratitude. So, we give until our *gratitude* is helped!

PRAYER: God, we need help in showing gratitude. We sense that we will feel more grateful once we start acting in a more grateful way, so move us to action! Amen.

Beggars Can't Be Choosers

SCRIPTURE: 1 Peter 1:18, 19

Have you ever heard the expression "Beggars can't be choosers"? What is meant is that anyone who is in need should be grateful for anything that is given. He or she should not question or resent the quality of what is given. The statement sometimes carries with it an air of contempt for the person in need. It conveys the feeling that a beggar is without dignity and power. Because this is true, people's remedy for beggars is usually in the form of scraps and leftovers--the easiest things to give.

God has never spoken to us who are spiritual beggars in that way. Though we are sinners, God remedied our situation by giving us the finest he could give...his Son! He gave from his abundance, not his leftovers. The offering we bring to God should reflect the best we have to give him, not the least!

PRAYER: Dear Lord, keep us from being cheap in what we give you. The temptation is sometimes great to short-change you, especially when things are tight. Keep us from hurting ourselves by being stingy. In Jesus' name. Amen.

Our Freewill Giving

SCRIPTURE: 1 Corinthians 16:1, 2

For almost 2000 years the church has been supported by the voluntary contributions of its members. People have supported the church financially because, in most cases, they have wanted to!

We can force people to do what they don't want to do for a short time. We can even pass legislation and for awhile coerce people to do things they would not normally like to do. But, in the long run, it is love and appreciation for a noble vision that causes people to include the church in their ongoing budgets.

We sometimes refer to the collection as a freewill offering. That is exactly what it is. It is support given freely and not our response to coercion. Our tithes and offerings are our way of taking seriously the words of Jesus: "Freely you have received, freely give!"

PRAYER: Lord, it is so nice to give when we don't have to. Thank you for making us want to do it! Amen.

The Mighty Mite

SCRIPTURE: John 3:16

Jesus honored a widow who gave a very small amount of money to God. This story in the Bible is usually referred to as the story of "the widow's mite."Jesus was honoring the proportion of her gift to the size of her wealth. The Bible says: "She gave all she had." Giving all that we have is giving the most anyone can give. When someone does that it is worth recording.

This is the entire point of the New Testament. The New Testament is what has been written down to remind us of what God has given. He gave everything he had! He only had one Son. God gave him to us!

The offering service is a very serious part of our worship service. It forces us to ask ourselves; "In the light of what God has already given, is our generosity all that it ought to be?"

PRAYER: God, the story of "the widow's mite" overwhelms me! The mite I give is not usually all I could give. Help me to gain the victory over my selfishness so I can give more of my all! In Jesus' name. Amen.

The Silver Exchange

SCRIPTURE: Matthew 25:35

With today's price of silver, I wonder what Judas would have received for betraying Jesus?

It sounds crass to put it this way, but this is the kind of question a person like Judas would ask himself. Whether we like to admit it or not, it is the kind of question we may unconciously pose to ourselves. It is easy to yield, as Judas did, to the temptation to exploit Jesus for whatever gain there might be. It is so easy to be a taker! It fits nicely into the jungle law of "the survival of the fittest."

The time in our worship service when we collect our tithes and offerings helps to temper the jungle code inside all of us. It teaches us the way of selfless concern for others. It reminds us that only through unselfish regard for others can the quality of our lives be improved. When we learn to give, we begin to live!

PRAYER: Dear Lord, we pray for more compassion for others. Help us to resist the temptation to overcome those with whom we compete and struggle. Help us believe in the survival of the giving! Amen.

Giving Up!

SCRIPTURE: Matthew 16:24-26

In the Tate Gallery in London, there is a famous painting by Frederic Watts with these words painted on it:

> That which I saved, I lost.
> That which I spent, I had.
> That which I gave, I have.

Jesus talked about the saving and losing of one's life. He said that by trying to save our life we will lose it and by losing it for God's sake we will at last save it.

No one can ever take away what has already been given away! A gift continues to bless the giver long after it has been given. If we deny ourselves the privilege of giving, we are robbing ourselves of the immediate satisfaction that giving can bring us, and also taking away the future joy that the memory gives when we recall those great moments of giving.

PRAYER: Creator God, we have saved and spent more than we have given. Help us to give up our old formula of selfishness for your prescription for life. Help us to give in to giving. In Christ's name. Amen.

Will Power and Won't Power

SCRIPTURE: Luke 6:29

There is an old story about the Sufi prophet, Nasrudin, who was approached by his neighbor to borrow his clothesline. Nasrudin said, "I cannot loan you my clothesline. I am drying flour on it!" The neighbor exclaimed, "I didn't know you could dry flour on a clothesline!" And Nasrudin replied, "It is amazing how many things you can do with a clothesline when you don't want to lend it out!"

If people do not want to make a contribution to the Lord's work, there is no limit to the number of excuses that can be found. On the other hand, if people want to share in extending God's kingdom, there is no limit to the reasons that will encourage them to do so.

We have never been in short supply so far as reasons or excuses are concerned. Stewardship comes down to *desire!* Do we want to give or don't we? People who want to give always find some way to do so!

PRAYER: Loving God, restore in us a desire to do more. Keep us from making lame excuses for not being generous. Help us to say, "I will!" In Jesus' name. Amen.

Keep It and You'll Need It

SCRIPTURE: Philippians 4:14-17

The Old Testament requirement of tithing is sometimes used as a guide to our giving today for supporting God's work. John H. Wells would often say: "If you *keep* that one-tenth you'll *need* it! Give it to God and see what God will do with it and with you!"

There is great wisdom in this thought. People are not attracted to stingy people. They are attracted to generous people. There is no great joy in helping or assisting people who are stingy. However, people are helpful and generous to people who are generous.

This reciprocity in kindness is one of the hidden reasons why our Lord encouraged generosity among his disciples. Asking us to give generously was his way of assuring us that we will be generously taken care of by others.

PRAYER: Lord, help us to trust in what generosity can do for us. Help us to rely on your promise that caring people will always be cared for. Grant us the courage to dispel our doubts with even greater acts of unselfish giving. Amen.

"One for the Money..."

SCRIPTURE: 2 Corinthians 5:1

As children we would sometimes say: "One for the money, two for the show, three to get ready, and four to go!"

I am not sure what this old saying means in its entirety, but a part of the meaning is quite clear. Before you can get going on most anything these days there is the matter of "money" that has to be considered.

Even Jesus had a treasurer in his small band of followers to handle the day-to-day requirements of his ministry.

While money may help in providing a beginning for our ministry we make it clear that money is not our end or goal. Our goal is spiritual and not material. We use the material in our attempt to show that God's realm is not of this world; the things of this world--even money--must be subordinated to it.

PRAYER: O Lord, keep our priorities straight in our lives. It is so easy to march to the tempo of the world's beat, and to find ourselves out of step with you. Take control of our money; take control of us! Amen.

Enthusiastic Giving

SCRIPTURE: Hebrews 12:1, 2

Do you remember the gifts that were brought to the Christchild when he was born? The magi brought him gold, frankincense, and myrrh. Do you remember what they brought him when he was dying? They gave him a crown made of thorns, a mock robe, and vinegar instead of water to drink when he cried out in thirst.

Judas had betrayed him. Thomas had doubted him. Peter and the rest of the disciples had fallen asleep as he prayed. The enthusiasm and excitement of the Bethlehem birthday had definitely diminished. And so had the size of the offering!

Our gifts to God are a measure of our enthusiasm. A dying church never needs more money. What it needs, more than anything else, is more enthusiasm for God's program. The church can always find some way of surviving without people's money, but it can never succeed without people's enthusiasm and good will!

PRAYER: Dear Lord, breathe in us a fresh spirit of joyous enthusiasm! Help us to become excited about the things that last and that improve the quality of life for all of us. Bring our financial commitment back to life again. In Jesus' name. Amen.

Inflationary Giving

SCRIPTURE: Genesis 12: 1-3

The thought of giving five percent, ten percent, or more of our income to God can be a frightening notion. *How could I ever get by on ten percent less?* we wonder to ourselves. And suddenly, inflation increases by ten percent and we endure it.

However, our ten percent "gift" to rising prices is not really a gift at all. It is a "bill." Because it is a payment and not a gift, we are robbed of the joy that comes from this kind of giving. No one is overjoyed when the price of something goes up!

But God has never inflated his demands on us. He is expecting no more or less from us now than he did from Moses and Abraham. And, furthermore, he promises us no less of a return on our investment of faith than he promised the patriarchs in the Old Testament.

So, we don't "pay" our tithes and offerings to God. We "give" them to him.

PRAYER: Father, inflate our interest and concern for your work. Create in us not only a clean heart but a big heart as well. In Jesus' name. Amen.

Being Generous to a Fault

SCRIPTURE: Romans 12:1, 2

Sometimes we hear a person speak of another as being "generous to a fault." The impression is conveyed that sometimes people can be too generous in what they give to others. This statement is not usually meant as a compliment. It is, at best, what is sometimes referred to as a left-handed compliment-- a gentle but definite put-down!

However, you never hear generous people criticizing generosity. Their regret is not that they give too much but, rather, that they do not give more. The generous person does not think of what could be done with the money, but, instead, thinks of what could be done if only more could be given.

If generosity is a flaw in one's character, then it is, indeed, an imperfection that God has used mightily in building and extending the kingdom throughout the world!

PRAYER: O God, how wonderful it would be if our greatest fault were our generosity! Help us all to be generous to a fault. If we make a mistake in our giving, help us to make it on the side of too much rather than on the side of too little. In Christ's name. Amen.

What's in a Name?

SCRIPTURE: Matthew 28: 19, 20

Shakespeare once wrote:

> "He who steals my purse steals trash;
> but he who robs me of my good name
> takes that which does not make him
> richer, but makes me poor indeed!"

We have no quarrel with the truth in this great statement. A purse can always be filled again, but a name that has been sullied by the thoughtless remark of another is not quickly or easily restored to its former luster.

However, what we do with the contents of our purse goes a long way toward defining the "name" by which we become known in the world. The names of King Midas and Scrooge remind us of greed and its destructive power in a person's life. A name like Carnegie, however, reminds us of the good that can come from hearts that are generous.

"What's in a name?" Shakespeare asked. A "name" is the sum total of the good deeds and the misdeeds of each of us. Sooner or later the purse plays its part in naming us for what we are!

PRAYER: Dear Lord, help us understand that we can change our name by changing the way we handle our material wealth. Amen.

Givers and Takers

SCRIPTURE: 2 Corinthians 9:6

The Sea of Galilee in Palestine has water flowing into it from the north and water flowing out of it from its southern shores. The Sea of Galilee is teeming with life. There are fish in its waters and birds building their nests in the trees at the water's edge.

The Dead Sea in Palestine, however, receives much water from the north, but it gives out no water at all from its southern shores. There are no fish in the Dead Sea. No birds build their nests there. This sea is quite appropriately named.

These two bodies of water are apt descriptions of the kinds of attitudes we often have toward our material blessings.

Some people are both "givers" and "takers," and usually these people are filled with a tremendous capacity for joy and life!

Others, however, are "takers" only. They are people who are more concerned with receiving and who know very little of the joy of unselfish giving to others. They know little of the truth of Jesus' statement, "I have come that you might have life and have it more abundantly."

PRAYER: O God, remove our "taking" attitude. Give us a "giving" spirit. Amen.

Diogenes' Cup

SCRIPTURE: John 14:18-20

Diogenes was a Greek philosopher in the fourth century before Christ who was known for his austere life. He renounced all his worldly goods except for one small silver cup from which he drank daily at the village fountain. One day he noticed a beggar cupping his hands at the fountain and drinking from the bowl of water his hands had formed. *I realize now that I don't actually need this cup any longer!* Diogenes said to himself. So he lived contentedly without the cup.

All of us have at least one Diogenes cup--something we think we simply cannot live without. But, as with Diogenes himself, none of the things we think are so essential to life are so important that they cannot be discarded. We still must learn the lesson Diogenes learned centuries ago: that we do not live by bread--or silver cups--alone! We have our hands and our heart of faith to sustain us at the fountain of life!

PRAYER: Dear Lord, help us to keep what we need and to discard what we don't. Help us to know the difference between the two! In Jesus' name. Amen.

Keeping the Change

SCRIPTURE: Philippians 4:13

Most of us, at one time or the other, have said to someone else: "Keep the change!" But we never say: "Keep the paper money!" Therein is the key to understanding this expression and to understanding ourselves as well. We don't mind too much if we relinquish small amounts of change to another. "After all," we say to ourselves, "it is no great loss to me!"

That which is no great loss to us is also no great gain to the other person either. If we have not diminished ourselves to any degree, then we have also not enlarged the other person. In short, we have not done the person any great favor!

In God's kingdom we try to overcome thinking in terms of "small change." Instead of asking; "What is the *least* I can give to get by with?" we should say to ourselves; "In the light of all that God has given to me, perhaps I should keep the change and trust God with the bigger part!"

PRAYER: Keep us Lord, from short-changing ourselves by giving only small change. Help us act in ways that make both us and your kingdom more vital. In Jesus' name, amen.

God, Our Only Guarantee!

SCRIPTURE: Isaiah 58:11

Sometimes you will hear someone comment that tithing one's income to God is "good business." That is, it is good for business. This kind of statement is meant to endorse tithing and to encourage other people to venture forth with faith into tithing.

However, we have to be very careful that our motivation for giving to God is a proper one. There are a lot of poor people who tithe. Many of them have tithed all of their lives--and they are still poor! There is no guarantee that by giving money to God's work our financial picture will be improved. It may get worse!

We have the promise, however, that God will never entirely forsake us. Tithing our money to God is an expression of faith, and like all acts of faith it is a response on our part that asks for no guarantees other than the promise of God's presence!

PRAYER: Lord, we are letting go of a small, but important part of our security--our money! We need your presence now; may our trust be more firmly placed in thee. Amen.

Dumb Barter

SCRIPTURE: Psalm 51:15

There is a quaint practice among certain primitive cultures of exchanging goods with other groups whom they dislike, or in some cases, with whom they are even at war. This practice is called "dumb barter." It is referred to as "dumb barter" because they do not engage in speaking or in conversation with one another. Each tribe simply places its goods to be traded in a prearranged location and returns the next day to find the items they need for survival. Sometimes this unusual practice of economic exchange goes on for years!

Each gift we give to the Lord should be a prayer or a statement of our faith in God. Our gift is an exchange we are making with God which makes both God and us richer. Our giving should not hinder or ever be a substitution for communication with God. Instead, it should encourage it. The blessings we receive are God's way of talking to us. Our tithes and offerings are one of the best ways we have of speaking back!

PRAYER: Creator God, listen to our offering speak for us. We hope its eloquence speaks well of us. We have much more to give because we have much more to say! In Jesus' name. Amen.

We Must Leave the Tip!

SCRIPTURE: Deuteronomy 8:10

When Jesus was dying on the cross he cried out: "It is finished!" The Greek word Jesus used was *tetelestai*, a term sometimes used among money lenders when a debt was paid. It means, literally, "Paid in full!"

There is no amount of money we can give God to secure our forgiveness and salvation! The debt has already been paid. Our financial support of the church's program is not for the purpose of securing a position for ourselves at God's side. That has already been done for us.

Our gift to God, then, simply represents the tip we are placing on the table. Our gift, like a tip, is our expression of appreciation for the good service God has provided us through the loving sacrifice of his son. And, like all tips we give, the amount we leave represents our gratitude and appreciation.

PRAYER: Dear God, we know that what we place in the offering today could be used to pay the bills or to purchase any number of trivial things. However, we have been fed so generously by your Spirit that we must express our gratitude. Our hope is that our good beginning will insure a good ending! Amen.

Penny Pinching

SCRIPTURE: Leviticus 23:22

There are numerous expressions we all know which encourage frugality--"A penny saved is a penny earned," and "A fool and his money are soon parted." The Bible, too, teaches that we are to be good stewards of every talent God has given us.

However, there is a thin line between frugality and stinginess. Stinginess describes someone who is not only tight with money, but who is tight with everything else he or she has as well. Stinginess is not just a way a person acts with money. It is a way of dealing with people. Stinginess not only closes one's purse to others, but it also closes one's heart. People are stingy because they do not have much heart.

We are asked by God to give generously and cheerfully from our financial resources, not because God needs our money but, rather, because giving to the needs of others is one of the best ways we have of knowing how much heart we actually have!

PRAYER: Merciful God, use our purse to open our hearts! Help us to give enough until it warms our concern for others. We know you have heart because you gave everything you had. Amen.

The Golden Rule

SCRIPTURE: 1 Timothy 2:1, 2

There is a principle the world lives by called "the golden rule."What the world means by this principle is; "Those who have the gold, *rule!*"

Christians live by a golden rule, too. However, what Christians mean by this principle is, "Those who have the gold, *share!*" To those of us who are Christian, the ultimate goal in life is not ruling but sharing!

When we bring our tithes and offerings to God, we are saying that it is not money that captures and rules our hearts and actions; it is sharing and caring. We acknowledge, by giving, that the God "who owns the cattle on a thousand hills" does not need more of our money as much as he needs more of our commitment to a life of sharing. God understands that only in this way will other people be led to an understanding that the golden rule has nothing to do with gold at all. It has to do with caring people taking advantage of every golden opportunity they have to share with others!

PRAYER: Dear God, help us to give away as much as we can possibly live without. Help us to show the world that we are not on the gold standard but on your standard! Amen.

Money Talks

SCRIPTURE: Malachi 3:10

We have all heard the expression: "Money talks!" What we usually mean by this statement is that money enables us to get our way. It enables us to get what we want!

We have all used money at one time or the other to talk our way out of a difficult situation. It is amazing how fluent we can become when we start flashing some money around! Money can overcome the barriers of language, age, and even great philosophical differences between people.

But if our own money talks, what is it saying? Is it saying: "Charity begins at home and you have to look out for yourself in this selfish old world!" Or, is it saying: "What's mine is yours, and more if you need it!"

If *our* money could talk about *us*, what would it say? The offering time should be the noisiest time in the worship service, because that is the time our money is doing the talking for us!

PRAYER: Lord, we are listening now to what our money is saying about us. We know you are listening too! We promise, you will be hearing more from us again. Amen.

The Midas Touch

SCRIPTURE: Luke 12:13-21

In Greek mythology Midas, the King of Phrygia, was granted a wish by the god Bacchus for having befriended him in an hour of great need. Midas asked that he be granted the power to change anything he touched into gold. For awhile Midas reveled in the joy of his immense new wealth, that is, until he became hungry and the food he touched turned immediately into gold!

Greed separates us from other people while generosity brings us closer to others! One of the serious consequences of greed is loneliness. One of the joyous consequences of a generous and sharing spirit is the warm friendship and fellowship that often follows.

Every Christian has the potential for a Midas touch. Each of us has the capability to touch and enrich a person with loving concern. Bringing tithes and offerings in worship represents one of these opportunities to "lay up for yourself treasures in heaven."

PRAYER: Generous God, we are here today because we have been enriched by your touch. Help us, through our giving, to touch others too! Remind us, from time to time, how greed can tarnish golden opportunities for good. In Jesus' name. Amen.

"Take No Purse with You!"

SCRIPTURE: Psalm 37:3

When Jesus sent the twelve disciples out on their first preaching mission he told them not to take any purse with them at all. They were to go forth with only faith in their hearts, faith that the words of Jesus would soften the hearts of the people who listened and opened their purse strings as well. Jesus said to them: "A laborer is worthy of his hire."

Not everyone has the talent or the inclination to enter the professional ministry. However, any person can play a vital role in God's ministry by financially contributing to the church's program to keep ministers and other church workers free from excessive worry over money matters.

While money does matter--and ministers and church workers need money too--other things matter more! It is up to us as Christians to take care of the purse of those who are called to God's ministry.

PRAYER: God, it is a wonderful thing to be a stockholder in the church's ministry! Help those of us who cannot preach to make possible the sermons that are preached, the marriages and baptisms that are performed, and the healings or cups of cold water that are given in Jesus' name! Amen.

Conspicuous Consumption

SCRIPTURE: Matthew 6:1, 2

In sociology there is a concept known as "conspicuous consumption" which describes a person who uses his money to buy things in a very flashy or showy manner. It is a way to be seen by people. Some of us have neighbors or friends like that.

Jesus said that in giving "our right hand should not know what our left hand is doing." It is not an easy thing for one hand to hide its actions from the other, or to keep our good deeds from being announced or conspicuously displayed for others to see. Our tithes and offerings should temper our arrogance and feelings of superiority, not arouse them. The only thing conspicuous about our spending should be the pleasure or joy we derive from being allowed to share in God's plan for enlarging the Kingdom. Your gift is for you to know, and for no one else to find out about!

PRAYER: O Lord, we are entering our closets now, not for prayer, but to make our contributions for your work. We are here, in secret, not to parade our gifts before others, but, to put them on display before you. Amen.

Giving Is Our Middle Name

SCRIPTURE: Luke 12:48

Jesus once said: "Where your treasure is, there shall your heart be also." Every lover knows the truth of that statement. The thing or person we value--our heart's treasure--has a way of capturing our soul, our mind, and our body! There is a very close proximity between heart and treasure.

That is why there is such a declaration of war when we try to separate someone from some habit or person he treasures. His entire being struggles against losing what has captured his heart.

For Christians, the giving of money for God's work should not represent a time of warring or conflict within us. "Giving" should be our "middle name" and our deepest desire. Because we have been given so much, the invitation to give to the Lord should be our most treasured experience!

PRAYER: Lord, most people know us by our first or last names. However, you also know us by our middle name. As we bring our tithes and offerings now, help us to live up to our good name. In Christ's name we pray. Amen.

Three Walnuts and Two Boys

SCRIPTURE: Proverbs 15:27

Someone once asked Abraham Lincoln what was wrong with his two sons who were crying, and Abe said; "What is wrong with them is exactly what is wrong with the entire world. I have three walnuts and each one of my boys wants two of them!"

Life is not at all fair! There are vast differences between people in their beauty, their intelligence, their health, and in their financial power. It is fortunate for us, however, that we are not judged by what we have received in life, but rather, by what we give. It is in giving, "as we have prospered." that we can become equal with all others.

We know we cannot count on life's being fair. But we also know that God is counting on our being fair by giving our fair share of what we have received. It is not important that some will give more or less than others. What is important is that when we give our *fair* share, life will become fair for us all, and we will become equal with one another!

PRAYER: Gracious Lord, through our giving and generosity we know we can become equal with all others. Help us to make life more fair by giving our fair share! In Jesus' name, Amen.

Blessed Are the Givers

SCRIPTURE: Luke 6:38

Someone once said, "It is more blessed to give than to lend, and it costs about the same!" Part of the joy of Christmas, birthdays, and anniversaries is the thrill of giving presents and watching the expressions of excitement and joy on the faces of those receiving them. It would be impossible to create such an air of excitement by "loaning" gifts on these special occasions. Such an idea would be silly.

God is not in the loaning business either. The Scriptures say: "He *gave* his only Son!" There is, indeed, profit to be made in making loans, but there is no joy. On the other hand, when you give generously, your financial reserves may diminish, but your happiness will increase! It is not only true that "God loves a cheerful giver," but it is also true that giving makes a person cheerful!

PRAYER: Lord, add to our pleasure as we bring our offerings. Help us to know that sometimes, when we have less left over, we end up with much more that we didn't realize would be ours! In Jesus' name. Amen.

Relevance and Reverence

SCRIPTURE: Ephesians 5:21

Enlightened social programs to help the widowed, the aged, the parentless, and the needy in general, did not originate with our American culture. These humanitarian programs were first instituted by the church 2000 years ago.

The church in the New Testament was never concerned with one's "spiritual" needs alone. For the church, the nature of a person's need always determined the nature of the church's service. If a person was hungry, the church fed her or him. If one was lonely, the church offered friendship. If one were caught up in the misery of guilt over sinful ways, the church preached repentence and forgiveness. It did not preach repentence to the hungry nor did it try to stuff the sinner with food.

How biblical a church is depends on how successful it is in meeting the needs--all of them--of God's people wherever encountered. The offerings and tithes we give the church help it be both relevant toward others and reverent toward God!

PRAYER: Dear Lord, keep us reverent by being relevant. Help us to touch our brothers and sisters in the way they need to be touched. Amen.

The Steward's Stewardship

SCRIPTURE: I Peter 4:10

We sometimes refer to our financial obligation toward God as our "stewardship responsibility." A steward in the Bible was an official who was given the responsibility to manage finances and possessions that belonged to another. He was to manage with the same care he would exercise if the possessions were his own.

Christians affirm the central truth that everything we possess--our talents, our time, and our treasury--is on loan to us. We affirm that all of these gifts will return to God some day.

While we are in possession of these grand gifts, we are commissioned by God to be good stewards of them. The tithes and offerings we bring each week are only a reminder that everything we possess is simply a gift that we enjoy for a while. Our stewardship, then, covers the entire amount God has given us. We dare not give ten percent to God's glory and ninety percent to someone else's glory! The amount we *give* reminds *us* of God's glory and goodness. The way we spend the rest reminds *others* of it!

PRAYER: O God, help us to be good stewards of what we have been given and of what we, in turn, should have given away. Amen.

Giving—a Way of Growing Up!

SCRIPTURE: Isaiah 58:10

The Apostle Paul once recorded some words Jesus spoke that were not written down by any of the four gospel writers. Paul quotes Jesus as saying; "It is more blessed to give than to receive" (Acts 20:35).

What a happy thought! In fact, the word "blessed" means "happy." It is the same word Jesus used when he spoke the beatitudes; "Blessed (happy) are the poor," and the like.

When we were children we felt that pure happiness was when we had received something. Childhood is an experience of receiving. This was exactly what Paul had in mind when he spoke to the Corinthian Christians; "Now that I have become a man I have put away childish ways."

There comes a time in all of our lives when we have to grow up! Giving is not only a sign we have grown up, it is also the prescription God has given to help us grow up. It is a way of helping us leave our childhood selfishness behind!

PRAYER: Dear God, it is embarrassing when grownups are told they must grow up! Help us to begin with our attitude toward giving and then to extend our growth to the other parts of our life as well. In the name of your adult Son. Amen.

Cash and Carry

SCRIPTURE: Matthew 6:33

It used to be quite common to see signs that would say; "Cash and Carry." The only way you could carry any goods away with you was for you to have the money to pay for what you needed.

Being able to say "Charge it!" has changed all of that. Many of us have learned that being able to purchase on credit can easily give us a false sense of buying power. The lesson behind credit purchases is that sooner or later we are forced to pay for the things we get to enjoy right away.

Our relationship with God is always "cash and carry." We cannot postpone our obligation to express our gratitude for what God has done for us. We cannot simply say; "Charge it!" and expect that God's blessings will continue to flow our way. It is our continuing expression of a debt of gratitude that helps to keep our account open with God!

PRAYER: Merciful God, there are thousands of forgotten moments when we should have said "Thank you!" Please accept these gifts as a way of opening our account with you once more. We want to carry away a greater blessing from you than we have known thus far. In Christ's name. Amen.

Giving Back the Overchange

SCRIPTURE: Romans 14:8

We have all had the experience of having been given back too much money in change for something we purchased. We remember the few seconds which followed when we debated the wisdom of making the clerk's mistake known and return the overchange. Some of life's ethical struggles come in seconds, not in hours, days, or years!

We might think of the offering we bring to God as returning some of his overchange. The love and forgiveness God has given us are far more than we will ever deserve. The presence of his guiding spirit is worth much more than anything we have ever given to God.

So, when we place our gift in the offering we may think of it as returning what we do not really need or have a right to keep. Let's think of all we give back as simply returning the overchange!

PRAYER: God of love, what we give you now is small change compared to what we are keeping back. Help us to add to the delight of our giving by remembering, from day to day, how much more we have received than we have given. Amen.

The Promised Land

SCRIPTURE: Romans 4:13

Tolstoi tells a story of a king who promised one of his favored servants all the land he could encircle in one day's time. So, on the appointed day, the servant started out as fast as he could run toward the East, and then circled toward the North and the West. Finally, when the day was almost over, the servant ran toward the South to close the circle of his promised land. When he reached his starting point he fell dead from exhaustion at the king's feet. The servant was buried in a piece of land six feet long by three feet wide. Tolstoi concludes, "This is all the land that any of us really needs in life."

It is not always easy to distinguish between our wants and our needs. Most of us want far more than we actually need. One of the reasons generous sharing in the church is important is to temper our wants and greed by focusing on what we all really need. Church is where we learn that the promised land is that land which is under our feet at any given moment when life is dedicated to God.

PRAYER: Lord, help us to know the difference between wants and needs and to be committed first to what we need. Amen.

Freely Given Is Not Cheap Grace

SCRIPTURE: Exodus 19:5

A father complained constantly about how much his son was costing him. There were school expenses, clothes to buy, and an automobile to keep up. Every expense by his son brought on a new round of complaints and criticisms. A friend said to the father one day, "My son doesn't cost me anything anymore. He died last week!" The complaining father was stunned and ashamed.

The things we value and prize in life cost us something. Nothing of any worth comes cheaply! God's grace and forgiveness are free to us, but they are not cheap. Someone had to pay a great price for the joy and peace we treasure.

The size of the offerings we give to God are a measure of how much we value God's gift to us. No one may know what the size of our offering is, at first, but in time, everyone will know because the gifts we give leave their mark on us.

PRAYER: O Lord, we all know we are marked men and women. Help us to know that the marks can be changed through offering opportunities. In Christ's name we pray. Amen.

Giving Is a Handout

SCRIPTURE: Romans 15:1, 2

You will sometimes hear people criticize the church because, in their words, "They always have their hands out for money." Seldom do these people stop and think that this is also true of the person who pumps their gas, the doctor who cures their ills, and the school which educates their young. They wouldn't expect free gas or free healing, but somehow they have convinced themselves that the riches of heaven shouldn't cost them anything at all.

These people probably never stop to think that gas stations, medical clinics, and local schools seldom, if ever, give their money away to help other places which are trying to meet the spiritual and physical needs of humanity. The church, however, gives much of its money away to help others.

So, the money we receive in the church is given twice. It is given once when we give it, and it is given again when the church responds to cries for our help. The church's hands are out so it can extend a helping hand to others!

PRAYER: Lord, our offering today is not a holdup as much as it is a handout! Help us to extend our hands to help those who are in need! Amen.

The Offering

SCRIPTURE: Exodus 25:2

We sometimes refer to the collection we take in our worship service as an "offering." An offering is something we offer God.

As God's children, we have offered God a variety of gifts to demonstrate our love and affection. We have offered grain, fruit, birds, various kinds of domestic animals, and money.

One consistent quality characterizes each of these gifts we read about in the Bible. Each gift represented the best someone had to give. People in the Bible always gave their firstfruits, the perfect lamb, never their leftovers.

In determining the character and amount of money we should give to the Lord, we must not ask, "What is the least amount I should give to be secure in God's kingdom?" Rather, we should say, "Because I am secure in God's kingdom, what is the most I can offer as a gift to God?"

PRAYER: Dear Lord, make our gift the best gift it can be. You know our financial circumstances. You know what we are wanting out of life. Help us not to lose a greater gift by offering a blemished one. In Jesus' name, Amen.

Keeping Up with the Joneses

SCRIPTURE: Acts 4:34, 35

Someone said, "It was fairly easy to keep up with the Joneses--until they refinanced!" There is tremendous pressure on all of us to measure our own worth and sense of self-esteem by what our neighbor possesses. When someone, for instance, asks the question: "How much is a certain person worth?" he is asking a question about money. It is very easy for financial holdings to become the definer of a person's worth.

Jesus spent much of his ministry trying to clarify the idea that his kingdom was "not of this world." He made it quite clear that one's bank account or stock holdings gave no one, not even the Joneses, an edge over anyone else.

The irony is, however, that while money can sometimes blind a person from seeing Christ's kingdom, money is also needed by the church to further its work of making Christ's kingdom more visible to those who seek it. In keeping up with the Joneses, we can lose sight of the most important things in life, or we can finance God's kingdom and remove the desire to keep up with anybody at all!

PRAYER: O God, help us to get out of the race of trying to keep up with others. Make us content in trying to keep up with thee. Amen.

Cheerful Giving

SCRIPTURE: 1 Chronicles 29:9

The Apostle Paul once said: "God loves a cheerful giver!" The word he used for "cheerful" was the Greek work *hilaros*. We derive the work "hilarious" from it. Paul was saying: "God loves the hilarious giver."

Giving to God should be a joyful experience! Giving is one of the ways in life by which we let the joy out. Joy is an extremely intoxicating emotion. Once it is experienced, more is desired. Giving to God and others is one of the most effective ways we have of releasing this wonderfully joyous sensation. This is, perhaps, one of the reasons why people who have learned to give generously are the last ever to want to stop giving in the way they do.

So--do something hilarious. Give generously! You will never feel the same again. That is, until you give the next time!

PRAYER: Dear God, we are stopping for a moment now to let the joy out. We have been told that you love these moments! Help us to learn to love them as much as you do. In Jesus' name, Amen.

Nickels, Dimes, and Dollars

SCRIPTURE: 1 Thessalonians 5:18

I overheard someone once make this remark about his children, "I wouldn't give you a nickel for another one, but I wouldn't take a million dollars for the ones I already have!"

Sometimes we forget how valuable are the people and things we have at our fingertips. When we are busy "using" them, they are worth a nickel! All of a sudden, when we are threatened with losing them, they are worth a million dollars to us.

The offering time is our time to change our thinking from nickels and dimes to thinking in terms of the highly-priced treasures we enjoy daily. It is a time to think of each other's love--a time to think of God's cleansing and forgiveness. It is a time to think of renewed hope for fresh beginnings. It is, indeed, a time to think of how richly we have been blessed. We are certainly millionaire saints, not nickel and dime ones!

PRAYER: Lord, help us to be in touch with the blessings of our vast resources and to give, not out of our poverty, but out of our plenty! Amen.

Giving: A Heart-To-Heart Experience (Christmas)

SCRIPTURE: Luke 2:20

Have you ever wondered why the wise men brought such expensive presents to the Christ child when he was born? It was not because they owed him anything.

The wise men were bringing favors, not returning a favor. They were showing their gratitude and appreciation for the most wonderful birth in all of human history. They were witnesses to the birth of God's Son! Their hearts were full of joy and wonderment at the richness of this miraculous moment. They knew that full hearts could not come empty-handed to the Son of God. They also knew that the giver's heart is always revealed by the giver's gift.

God had laid bare his own heart when he gave us the best he had--his Son. The Wise Men did the same with their costly gifts. Our tithes and offerings at Christmas must represent the best we can offer God. Then Christmas becomes a heart-to-heart experience.

PRAYER: O patient Lord, we know that when you look at our offering you see our heart! It is frightening to bare ourselves like this, but we know of no other way to experience what the wise men enjoyed. We give the best we can, and receive the best you offer. Amen.

Having the Time of Our Lives! (New Year)

SCRIPTURE: Proverbs 11:25

All of time is broken into chunks! We can speak of eons of time and millennia of time, but most people would rather think and talk in terms of days, weeks, months, years, and decades of time. And for most of us, having one day each year when we can begin counting time all over again from zero is a helpful thing. New Year's Day gives us the feeling of a fresh new start. The new year gives us another opportunity to be better stewards of our time.

Our money is also broken into chunks! We can speak of millions and billions of dollars, but most of us are more comfortable with thinking in terms of hundreds and thousands. We have all lost and wasted money in the same way we have lost and wasted time. The new year gives us a fresh start with our time, and provides us with a fresh look at the way we use our money. Giving generously to God's work can truly help us to have "the time of our lives."

PRAYER: Dear Lord, give us a greater resolve to use both our time and our money more wisely. Help us to know how important the use of money is in determining the quality of our life. In Jesus' name. Amen.

Words Are Cheap!
(Palm Sunday)

SCRIPTURE: James 2:14-17

When Jesus rode into Jerusalem in the final week of his life, a crowd witnessed his triumphal entry into the city and shouted with a loud voice, "Blessed is he who comes in the name of the Lord" (Mark 11:9). Less than a week later, a crowd cried out to Pilate, "Crucify him! Crucify him!"

Crowds are fickle! They are irrational too. People can be moved by the pressure of many to cry out "Hosannah!" but, in a crowd, words are cheap! In a crowd people can escape the individual responsibility for what the crowd says or does.

Jesus does not call crowds to repentance; he calls individuals. We cannot turn to the crowd and have it fulfill our responsibilities before God. We must do that all alone. Giving our tithes and offerings to God cannot be a "crowd" experience. It is a solitary experience. We are judged by our generous efforts, not by our generous words. We put our money where the need is!

PRAYER: Father, we know we cannot let the person next to us do our giving or our speaking for us. We know we have to do that ourselves. Help us not to be cheap, either in what we say or in what we give. In Jesus' name. Amen.

The Resurrection--an Unexpected Dividend (Easter)

SCRIPTURE: Luke 6:38

One of the interesting aspects of the resurrection of Jesus is the element of surprise. Everyone in the Easter story--the women, the disciples, the two strangers on the road to Emmaus--was surprised!

Surprises keep life from being predictable! The things we can predict we can control. Surprises keep us from controlling the events around us, and put us in the position of being controlled. A person who can be controlled is a person who can be used by God.

All of us, at one time or the other, have received money we never expected to receive, an unexpected dividend. Many people who tithe their incomes regularly tell of experiences where they have been surprised by financial blessings in their lives. Giving a proportion of our income to God is very similar to the first Easter experience. Our offering is buried in the collection plate, and from all outward appearances it is gone. But then, as in the first Easter, it comes back to us in many different forms to bless and encourage us. What a surprise and what a blessing giving to God can be!

PRAYER: Lord, take our gift and surprise us! Help us to believe again that nothing given to you is ever lost nor does it ever go unrewarded! Amen.

Giving Is a Balancing Act (Mother's Day)

SCRIPTURE: Proverbs 3: 9, 10

Most mothers believe in the principle that lies behind biblical tithing, that is, *reciprocity*. They believe that much of life is regulated by how well one balances the giving to and the taking from others. They understand better than most that sooner or later one is rewarded for one's efforts on behalf of others.

Mothers are highly honored, not because they are intelligent, wise, or beautiful, but because they are givers. It was once said of Elizabeth Barrett Browning, "It was her thinking of others that made you think of her!"

The size of our offerings on Sunday is a good indication of how well we have learned the lesson of unselfishness from our mothers. The mother who filled our plates as children would urge us to fill the collection plates as adults, balancing our generous receipts with our generous gifts!

PRAYER: O God, when we honor our mothers, we honor you! We honor the difference a giving person can make in a world that is busy taking. Help our giving today to restore some balance in life. Amen.

The Church Which Has Everything (Pentecost)

SCRIPTURE: Psalm 41:1

We have all faced the problem of what birthday present to buy for the person who has everything. We may also wonder what we should give to the church on its birthday when the church already has so much.

We must remember that the quality of our gift should not be determined so much by the person or place receiving it as by the person giving it. We should not give beggars less because they have less, nor should we give kings more because they have plenty. Giving should be a reflection of our love and gratitude toward God and not a reflection of the church's bank balance.

While people should be responsive to the many needs to which the church ministers, our greatest need is to see ourselves as giving people. The church deserves our love, our loyalty, our time, our talent, and our treasure.

PRAYER: Lord of life, we confess that our need to be givers is even greater than anyone else's need to receive what we give. We know the world could somehow survive without receivers, but we know that it could never survive without givers. Help us to give to help those who are really in need...*ourselves*! Amen.

Healing a Father's Hurt
(Father's Day)

SCRIPTURE: 1 Peter 2:9

Some of us can remember when our father took us to the woodshed or to the back room for some wrong we had done. We can also, perhaps, recall him saying something like, "This is going to hurt me more than it does you!" We recall how well he bore up under the pain and how well we didn't!

Fathers, however, sometimes bear a great deal of pain in rearing their children. It is often a pain they don't talk much about. Fathers go without things they need so their children won't have to. They pretend to "like" such things as chicken necks and wings because their children prefer the meatier parts.

Some things hurt a father more than they do his children. The thing that hurts the most is an ungrateful heart, especially the heart of an ungrateful child! Persons who are generous and grateful are good examples for all of us, but they gladden most of all a father's heart!

PRAYER: Father, we seek to gladden your heart by our gratitude. Keep us from inflicting hurt by being ungenerous. Help us to think of the offering as a good discipline for all of us. Amen.

Freedom Isn't Free (Independence Day)

SCRIPTURE: Galatians 5:13

Freedom isn't free! The price a country pays for freedom is the lives which are lost, the resources that are used up, and the money that is spent. But, as great as the cost of freedom is, it is not nearly so costly as is the loss of freedom. Slavery and tyranny are far more costly than is the quest for freedom.

The price that God paid for our redemption and freedom was extremely high. However, God understood that the alternative to losing his Son was to lose the entire human race. He realized that losing his Son for awhile was preferable to losing the rest of us forever!

The money we place in the offering week by week can never pay God back for what he has done for us, but it can remind us of the high cost of freedom.

PRAYER: Dear Lord, we know there is no charge for admission to the worship service today, but we also know there is a price we must pay if we are to get anything out of it. Help us to know that anything we value costs, and when we don't pay the price, we may lose what we most treasure. Amen.

Thanks for the Memories (Memorial Day)

SCRIPTURE: Isaiah 49:14-16

When Bob Hope sings his theme song, "Thanks for the Memories," he is expressing the joy that most of us have in recalling the pleasantness of the past. However, our memory is not always a selective instrument. When we turn it on, it recalls both the happy and the sad times, our victories and our defeats. Our memory is often like a turned-on faucet. It gushes forth our most sublime moments, and our silliest ones too!

The world spends much of its time remembering. So does the church. Most of what we do in our worship service is designed to help us remember past sacred events and our current sacred obligations as well.

When we invest our tithes and offerings in the church's program, we are saying to the world, "The church stands for something worth remembering!" The offering we give is our way of saying; "Thanks for the memories!"

PRAYER: O Lord, grant that our gift insures that the world will not forget what happened 2000 years ago. If it is important enough for us to remember, it is important enough for everyone to remember. Amen.

Indian Givers (Thanksgiving)

SCRIPTURE: Psalm 100

Thanksgiving is a holiday we celebrate each year to remind us of an important lesson we learned from the American Indians. It is the lesson of sharing! The early American settlers would have perished had it not been for the kind generosity of the Indians who befriended them in their first cold winter in the new country. The Indians gave food, and the settlers gave thanks! Everyone was giving something! When *that* happens, one turns it into a holiday. And we are still celebrating it today--a day of thanks for *giving*!

Every Lord's Day is the Christian's thanksgiving day! It is a day we stop and remember how greatly God gives, and how we must give thanks ourselves. It is not just a holiday for us; it is a holy day. We remind ourselves in our worship that there is no survival for any of us without generous giving and generous expressions of gratitude on our part. What we give to God will help us get through winter, and through life as well!

PRAYER: Generous God, this holiday is one Christians understand. Help us to remember how giving keeps everyone alive! Amen.

Worker's Compensation (Labor Day)

SCRIPTURE: John 4:35, 36

A prevailing view of work in the Old Testament was that work was punishment given humankind for Adam's sin. Much of Protestant theology, however, has redefined "work" as the way through which one can know whether he or she has been elected by God. According to some Protestants, work becomes one's ministry for God. This view is reflected in the adage: "An idle hand is the devil's workshop!"

There is a great difference between making a living and making a life. Some people work only to make a living. Some people's work, however, improves the quality of life for everyone. Jesus did not make a very good living, but he produced a wonderful life!

When we place our offering in the offering plate we are joining hands as fellow laborers in the world's most noble work. We will not get a raise for what we do, but we will be raised to life for it!

PRAYER: Dear God, thank you for the noble work you have called us to do. Accept this money we have earned from making a living, and use it to make over many lives! In Jesus' name. Amen.

Index by Scripture Reference

(Numbers in parentheses refer to pages in book)

Colossians 3:15 (11)
1 Thessalonians 5:18 (50)
1 Timothy 2:1,2 (31)
Hebrews 12:1,2 (20)
James 2:14-17 (53)
1 Peter 1:18,19 (12), 2:9 (57), 4:10 (40)